GW00870054

UPS AND DOW
TRUTH ATT.......
LIFE CONFIDENTLY

Katie Seco

Dear Sheeen,

Hope you enjoy it! :)

love Katie xxx

<u>Ups and down's: The truth</u>
<u>attaining life confidently</u>

For all who have helped me on
my journey to success.

Ups and down's: the truth about attaining life confidently

Prologue

Hello! Welcome to my prologue and journey to a successful (well hopefully!) path and snippet of my recovery of mental and physical health. With any luck, this poetry collection will allow for some shred of light into my own personal life, but also for emulating a more positive outlook on life generally. Things in this collection can be about anything you associate the words with, therefore hoping to put a smile on your face and ultimately show you that you CAN successfully get through life with my little words. The health system can be hard, but I have learnt a vast amount of knowledge and by putting it all into practice I have been able to access and tap into my own creative writing style (which I love, by the way) getting me to be confident in my own life, and overall hoping to make you feel more positive, subsequently causing you to be more comfortable and confident in what life throws at you, whether they be lemons or apples for example, you can apply these positive and empowering prose to help you which is...

My ultimate goal!

Katie x

Contents Page:

That Mask

Things are black,

Things are bleak,

Life stuck in here feels like being on a screen,

Watched and watched,

Every day's the same routine:

Meds, therapy, lunch and dinner,

But I do all this so I'm a winner!

Focusing on discharge, seeing friends and family,

But staying strong can get harder and harder,

However, striking that gong, putting my words into song,

Preparing for life onwards fighting strong.

It's okay to make mistakes,

It's okay to feel like you cannot try,

...but darling, you know what?

It's okay to cry,

It's okay to be a mess,

Just don't give up sweetheart, there is sunshine well within.

Strive for happiness, strive for love, that is all that matters above…

I know a smile can hide a thousand feelings and words,

But you, by cracking that mask,

You will have made that first step,

…to an amazing breakthrough,

Warriors are what we are,

Within and within appearance,

But being strong, I know is hard to do,

But I promise you, it is time.

Things can seem bleak,

But hey honey, you will make it in all honestly,

Hold my hand,

Take a breath,

Walk a few steps forwards, don't worry I've got your back,

We'll cross that finishing line in record time,

Finding happiness, feeling content, is what it's about.

We've done it darling,

We've done it sweetheart,

Cracked that mask is what you've done,

Forever replacing it with that radiant smile,

... and a free spirit is what you've become!

Life is like roots of a rose

Life is like roots,

Not the miniscule rose flower,

It takes courage,

Like tough old boots,

Determination and power...

But when your roots have grown massively,

Just think of that brilliant possibility,

That you'll have stability,

Within the ground.

Your rose will grow fully tall,

Beautiful and all,

Just like the roots underground,

Which will inevitably be able to withstand,

Anything thrown in its way,

Making your roots and flower,

Have infinite fire-power...

Just like that rose's now ever-thick roots,

You will be able to withstand all too!

The swirling winds

The wind howls,

The wind swirls,

All around,

Prowls.

It feels consuming,

Encompassing our every being,

Wrapping us up like a cocoon,

Threatening our every well-being.

The wind squashes us up,

Trapping us up in a constricted cage,

However, buttercup, don't worry,

It is only temporary,

This is only one book page,

The next is awaiting...

The endless struggle

Struggles are inevitable,

That is just life,

Ups and downs try to pin us all down,

But honestly, you can beat this all without a frown,

Even if it is just a slight curl of your lips upwards,

You are winning,

So, keep on swimming...

That goal can seem like forever,

Faraway, faraway, just far,

Keep going, even if it only your personal parr,

You will progress,

Keep on picking up those magical affirmations from your inspirational jar,

And you will not regress...

Up and down,

Things may seem f******** up,

But don't give up,

Throw your beautiful hair backwards,

Hold up your plaque,

That says, "I'm never giving up again…"

And ride that marching on train!

Fear and anxiety's grip

Fear, anxiety, can cause numerus problems,

The aim is to feel it and then manage it successfully,

Cope with it appropriately, therefore moving forward in, guess what?

Your recovery!

Fear,

Anxiety,

The 'great' dynamic duo,

 Are hard to eradicate, as this is near on impossible,

As it is part of human flaws or life,

But one day,

Someone unexpected will, one of the greatest, will stand right by your side.

The effects of those terms can be life threatening,

But that person will hug you, tightly, so you cannot breathe,

And you will slowly see…

Those puzzle pieces of joy and happiness can be glued in and taken over,

Protecting you from those more unpleasant emotions,

Set in those notions,

Keep in fast motions,

And cross those lonesome oceans...

You can do this!

Where, why, how?

Things can be very complicated,

Things can be grave.

Things can be gaited,

But you can be brave.

You have the power,

To change your ways,

It might not be easy,

But keep surfing the wave.

Try your hardest,

Things will improve,

Be your own artist,

Ad things will move.

Keep going in the right direction,

Fight for the best,

Look at your reflection,

And manage your near impossible quest.

The quest is your overall goal,

Keep it your mission,

Stay in control,

It is now your fruition.

You'll be alright

Don't stop,

Don't stop musing,

Keep trying your hardest,

Things will eventually go your way.

Keep dreaming,

Dreaming of what could happen,

Don't think completely in the past,

Overcome and let that go fast.

Fight. Fight. Fight...

You'll get to that place where you're ultimately alright!

You

You are you,

Nobody else has ever walked in your shoes,

Don't be ashamed,

For your past mistakes and mishaps,

For you, are you, the most important person in your life.

End of.

Keep moving forwards, one step in front of the other,

And you will keep heading toward freedom and eternal joy,

Keep that smile on your face,

Don't hide behind that brick wall of a mask,

I want you to be as happy as you can,

Despite your past circumstances.

But guess what?

Don't be ashamed at all, as,

YOU ARE YOU.

When things don't go your way

When things don't go your way,

Look up to the sky and say,

I'm not going to let you beat me down,

I'm going to wear my winning crown!

Stand up!

Stand up!

Stand up and fight!

You can go this, sweet,

Everything's 'gonna be alright,

Set your mind ablaze,

Remember this phrase,

Dust yourself off...

Get out of that negatively embracing ditch,

And say...

"You hit like a b****!

Darkness is not infinite

When things seem bleak and black,

Thing's may seem like this fact...

The world is a dark and scary place,

But keep up that fight

...fight 'till you, again, see the radiant sunlight!

Chambers of the mind

The mind is full of chambers,

These rooms, those hallways, that and those doors.

Finding that appropriate mechanism which will unlock,

A specific door.

This door will potentially have the power to change your life for eternity,

However, that correct door can take a long time to find.

But with perseverance and encouragement from other, as well as yourself,

You will eventually locate it,

You will find the exit,

And you will find the way out of the puzzling chambers of your mind.

You are beautiful

Just think,

Think hard,

You are beautiful end of.

You may think opposite,

But it not what is on the outside,

It is from what glows from within.

It doesn't matter whether you are wearing makeup,

Wearing expensive clothes,

Your beauty is from inside and is what exudes out.

The invisible shield

Autumn leaves are falling,

Falling to the ground with passers-by crunching them loudly,

Comfy big coats are worn,

Fluffy boots are dressed to impress,

The darkness coming to adorn,

Encompassing the little shred of light that again tries to take over.

We have pitched black shadows all surrounding us,

Our body and mind tell us that we are safe,

Safe from the darkness,

Never alone ever in our mind of chambers,

Providing us a safety net, of many doors to hide,

And the saviour, so to speak, love.

Love surrounds us just like the leaves trying to engulf us,

Our bodies, and mind, is saved due to love, so you see, it is like an invisible shield,

Getting us through one dimness or darkness to the ever-shining shield: Light.

We are on the path of safety and protection.

Progression and Growth

Things can seem bad,

Making us feel blue and sad,

Encompassing us in a lonesome ditch,

Making us switch and twitch.

People don't believe me when I say:

It can get better and you can have your way.

Previous to this stanza, I would have said,

There's no light at the end of this tunnel,

I'm holding on just be a diminishing thread...

Obscurity and unapologetically,

The wind howls all around,

Crowding and flocking,

Not making a bare sound.

Just picture this, this screaming darkness that was formerly a
silent and hushed,

Like a load of wrapped rope around your waist,

You find it hard to break free and ultimately breathe.

Like that, with the help of therapy, staff, friends and family,

I know that we're going to become us again easily,

Well maybe not easy, so per say, but steadily and surely,

Striving for perfection and growth is vital,

Follow these steps to success, therefore this will always be your running title!

The coping mechanism of crying

When people see you cry,

Don't be afraid,

It's okay, it's in order to get by.

Crying is okay,

It shows that you are only human,

Human enough to feel.

If others see your tears,

You don't have to be ashamed,

Crying is only natural and accepted,

So let them immediately flow,

Just let go.

Release that blustering backlog of emotion,

Let it all out,

All for progression…

...and you'll release your inner hero,

Making ad showing that you are mighty strong!

Friendship

Friendship is full of trust,

That is a massive must.

Having someone who you can speak to daily,

Is like a magic wand belonging to a fairy.

Talk to that special person,

Cry it out if you must,

Things may not worsen,

It can get better if you have a chat, or a hello,

Hugs are superior,

So keep them dear and near,

Forever...

Friendship can be described as a rainbow,

Maybe things are a bit messed up,

But guess what,

Look up,

Trust me,

Look up and you'll see that things can get better,

'specially if you have those adored people in your life.

Just a quick hello can be all that is needed to get you out of that dark place,

So keep the faith,

Carry on and fight,

Look up at that sign,

A rainbow will brighten,

You have the power to seize,

Don't sink down on your knees,

Giving up is not an option anymore,

Fight through and through,

'Cos you are the one.

Beauty/Perfection

Beauty.

Perfection.

This is just a recipe for disaster,

Beauty ones from within,

Perfection is unattainable,

Unachievable in fact.

Real beauty is not what you wear, how you act,

But it is what is on the inside.

Please, love, remember that important fact,

You are you and that is *real* beauty!

Perfection is not goal you will achieve,

It will only hold you back,

So steady on your feet,

Look into that lying, distorted mirror and say:

I am impeccable, OK?

Whatever size you are,

Whatever shape you fit,

You are you and this eternal beauty, not from perfection,

...but from the interior,

So pick up that flower, which you would associate with pure beauty, and tell yourself the same.

I AM BEAUTIFUL.

Stick with people who give a s***

People come in many different types,

Loud, quiet, lively and more,

But make sure you feel comfortable,

Because, one person it only takes, can shake your core.

Stick with people who care about your flaws,

Your boundaries,

As this is vital for complete companionship to work,

This is an immense perk.

Keep and allow yourself to trust,

But only when your values are not affected, this is a must,

However if these happen to be broken and not upheld,

You need to burn those bridges as fast as you can.

Trust is earned but once destroyed, it is hard again to gain and accordingly plan.

Stick with people who give a f***,

Otherwise you'll be surrounded by muck,

Keep those dear close to your heart,

Even if you are miles apart.

Keep your head up,

If you still have not found your crowd,

Keep your values, priorities and boundaries secure,

And you never know,

You will find your personal friendship or loving score,

Without a s****** messy war!

Hope

Hope is what we all need to hold on to,

Otherwise fear and anxiety will wipe it right out,

But do what you need, scream and shout,

Don't hold doubt,

Just remember that old saying "Hold On Pain Ends,"

Pushing you forward to transcend.

Grab that thing that you associate with positive vibes,

Whether that be a pen and paper, writing, art,

Just savour the moment, do some mindfulness, or
brainteaser puzzle,

Ultimately hope will escalate yet again.

Keep hope alive,

Stick positive post stick notes all round your room and mirror,

You'll feel clearer,

Nearer to that goal (don't forget),

STRIVE

41

MY INSPIRATIONS:

Lottie's Scream

Seeing you from the start,

I would never have believed,

A girl, like you, I would never have thought,

You'd be where you are now, shaping your dreams,

From that dismal, dark place,

Where you laid for eternity,

You fought so hard you fought so many battles, it was beyond belief.

I never lost faith, but I always wandered...

...is this girl going to do what she wanted?

Lottie, my dear, I am so immensely proud of the progress you have reached,

You strived so hard, never letting anything stop you, I preach,

Getting out of the toughest places ever observed,

So just like that, I thought, this girl is well deserved.

I just wanted to show you how proud I am of you,

How lucky I am to have you as an amazing friend,

Pal, you're one of the toughest cookies I've ever met.

Along my journey,

You inspire me every day,

Shining those radiant rays, along my way,

Making me strive whilst also emulating your own success.

From that dismal, dark place,

Where you laid for eternity,

You fought so hard you fought so many battles, it was beyond belief.

I never lost faith, but I always wandered…

…is this girl going to do what she wanted?

The journey has not been smooth,

Countless ups and downs,

But now, seeing you where you are,

Makes me awe you from afar,

You're keeping me on track,

Believing in me, makes me appreciate the fact, that,

Your cry is astonishingly ferocious!

So, keep that within,

You're going to amazing things!

For those who have helped me in my journey, I have written some prose to give you all a massive THANK YOU!

Just wanted to show you all how much of a massive difference you have made to my life and making me feel more confident in the path attaining recovery in my mental health and physical health journey!

Some of you may have gathered with this little book, I have been through some tough times and struggles, but having the space to write and write, whether it be poems, art, studying for my Paramedicine Foundation year for university, this has helped me focus on not engaging with maladaptive and negative coping mechanisms.

I am not ashamed of who I am. I am me. I am flawed. I am not perfect.

I am beautiful and loved and someone who is learning to accept herself even in her darkest days.

What I'm trying to say is:

You are you. There will be ups and downs in life, but you can attain confidently, taking back your life!

Here below are a few individuals who have helped inspire me to get better. With all of their help and determination with my absolute stubbornness, sometimes, they have managed to crack that mask slightly, allowing me to be myself.

Thank you, M!

Dear M,

Just thought I'd write you a poem to show them,

The amazing work you have done,

As well as making things here more fun,

Allowing us to learn the skills and skills,

We all need in order to move on!

Discharge seems more thought through,

Working with us profusely to...

... motivate us, and me, to keep on fighting and fighting,

So we can continue,

To find the proceeding plans and finding myself,

In for my own world!

Saying 'sorry' is now banned because of you, E, J and S,

But I continue to fight to use this word even less,

You are very knowledgeable and will succeed,

In everything you set your mind on to proceed,

Yours, as well mine, our futures will be bright.

You have helped me in more ways to fight,

Keeping strong is what I'm going to do, because of you,

Just remember you are smarter and will flourish,

To become that person with will astonish!

I wish you all the best,

For your success,

Keep going,

You will be glowing!

Radiant rays you will emulate,

So do not speculate...

... your abilities are one of a kind,

Just wanted to say,

Thank you for helping my mind to unwind!

Thank you, S!

Thank you, S, for all that you have done,

Helping me when I was literally undone,

Through your groups and groups with J and M,

Learning skills, making it more fun!

Your laugh is infectious,

It makes me smile,

S, you have believed in me for a long while,

Banning me as well, for saying 'sorry,'

It has made my mind flurry,

You more bluntish tone, when I catastrophise,

Brings me back down to realise,

That my thoughts were a tiny bit wild

You're one of a kind, with trust intertwined,

Your future is bright,

You are going to take flight,

Over and over, getting me to realise what is right.

Never losing faith in me,

Is what makes you special,

Guiding me without being judgmental.

This is what is needed in life, really,

As many people you meet may have complex problems,

But you I believe, will help them in volumes.

I have very faith that you will grow to be one of the most successful persons, I guarantee,

Cracking that mask is what you will have done,

For me, cracking that mask is what you have started to become,

Starting and helping me to replace it with a more radiant smile...

... and a freer spirit is what I have started to become!

Thank you, J!

J, thank you for all that you have done,

I was existing in a dreary nightmare,

I have practically won,

Well I'm getting there, well not nowhere...

anymore,

Thanks to you, J, I am finding my own way,

Working my way 'round that dark twisted path, hooray,

I was struggling immensely before you become one of my therapists,

And I never thought I'd become my own advocate,

You have taught me skills and skills,

That I am slowly starting to believe,

Using your guided hand,

I'm starting to achieve.

My dreams are gradually coming true,

Mostly due to you,

And that horrid black hurricane,

I was stuck in between,

Whirling all around,

Finding it hard to leave!

You are one smart lady,

Helping me with all of your heart,

Thank you so much with all of my heart.

Just overall, I want you to know,

You are going to go on to do the most amazing things,

Dazzlingly like the sun,

In my mind and heart, with skills and laughs,

Helping me to reach my end path!

So thank you, J,

For all that you have done,

Fighting my corner,

For me to develop into the adult who's coping more and more,

Gradually allowing me to run,

Now chasing my dreams for me to become,

Expressing positivity, from you,

I will definitely make it through!

Just some quotes to stand by:

You are you!

No one is perfect!

Beauty is from within!

Hold On Pain Ends (HOPE)!

Ride that turbulent storm!

All emotions are valid!

Keep strong; you're a warrior!

Just keep up that fight!

...and most importantly:

It's okay to not be okay....

Lots of love, hope this poem
collection has help emulate
positivity and exude
confidence,

Katie Seco x

Thoughts of your own/doodles: